What Is A California Gray Whale?

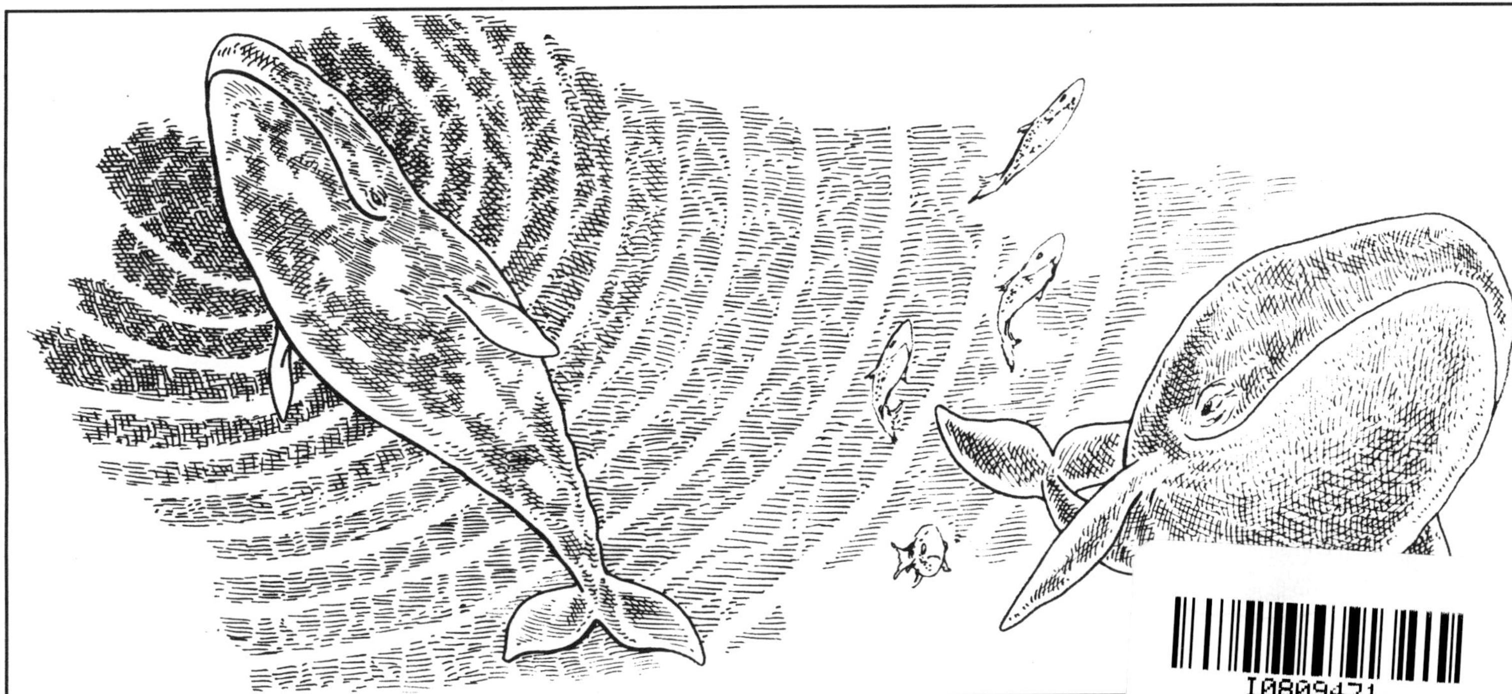

Written by Jack A. Graves **Illustrated by Cameron K. Daines**

The author expresses his appreciation to Mr. Paul W. Wild of the California Department of Fish and Game (Monterey office) for critiquing the manuscript and offering valuable suggestions.

Library of Congress Cataloging-in-Publication Data

Graves, Jack A.
What Is A California Gray Whale? / written by Jack A. Graves;
p. cm.
Summary: Examines the history, life, migration, and protection of the California gray whale.
1. Gray whale—Juvenile literature. (1. Gray whale. 2. Whales.)
I. Daines, Cameron K., ill. II. Title.
QL737.C425G72 1991 599.5'1—dc20 91-38038
ISBN 0-929526-13-9 (pbk.) : $4.95 CIP

American Educational Press
(a division of Double B Publications)
4113 N. Longview
Phoenix, Arizona 85014
(602) 274-7236

Printed in the United States of America
Second Printing with Revisions 1998

FOREWORD

I was pleased and honored to be asked to write the foreword for this author's latest children's book. While I was a student at California State University, Stanislaus, Dr. Graves was my professor for many reading courses where I learned much about the techniques used to teach elementary youngsters to master and then to enjoy the diverse world of literature. In his previous book about the California sea otter, he used significant information complemented by delightful illustrations. His current book on the California gray whale is equally informative, fun to read aloud to very young children, and can be read easily by boys and girls in the third grade and above. It is expertly illustrated with pen and ink drawings which add authenticity to the text.

The author's frequent journeys to coastal areas and his love of nature provide him with an appropriate background. I appreciate how he encourages environmental awareness and concern for the creatures of this earth. Educators will discover that this book is filled with useful terminology, as well as fascinating and incredible facts. With our current ecological concerns, the author has created a gem of a book that is a pleasure to read and which provides a useful introduction to one of the giant wonders in the world of mammals. I am confident that teachers, parents, and most importantly, children, will find this book an enjoyable reading experience.

Kevin W. Wychopen
Elementary Teacher
Sonora School District
Sonora, California
October, 1991

Especially for my young friends Noelani and Beau

A California gray whale is a large mammal that lives in the ocean.

It belongs to a group of whales known as baleen. The baleen whale has been discovered as having existed as long ago as thirty million years!

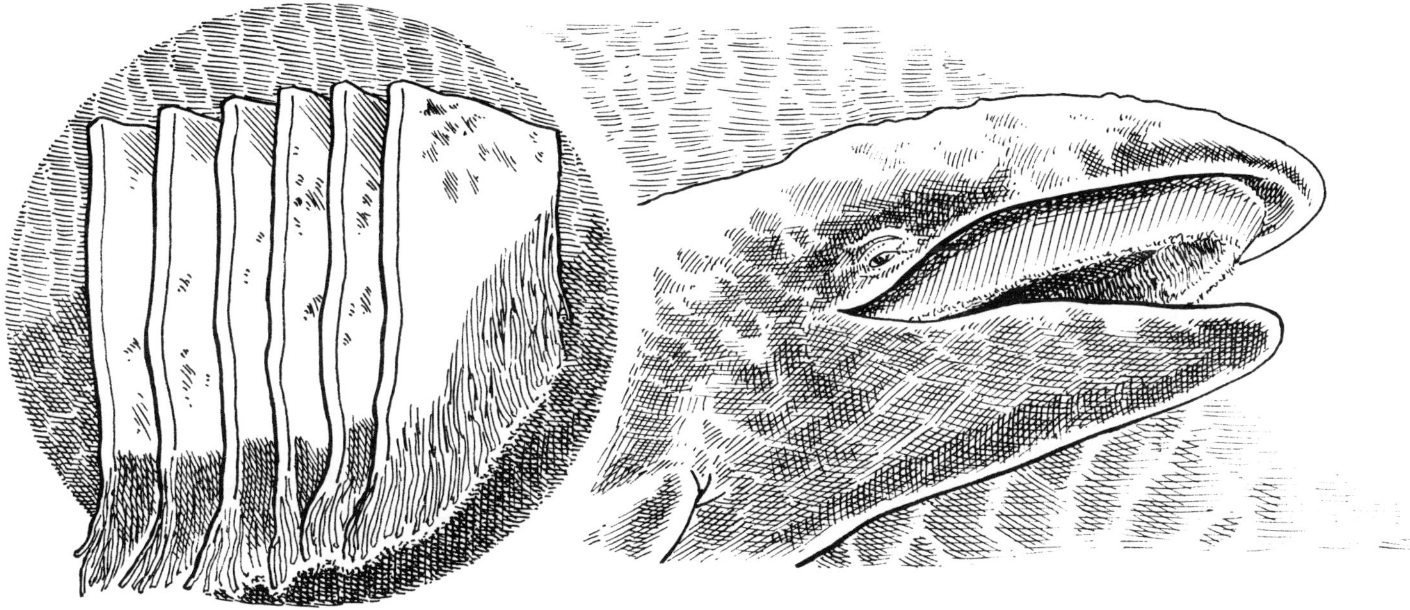

Baleen, called "whalebone," hangs from the upper jaw of these whales where teeth are usually located. This horny material has many hairlike fibers located on the inner side. These fibers serve as a kind of sieve to filter the food from the water.

In the days of whaling, many years ago, baleen was made into cooking utensils, brushes, and other kinds of practical items.

Surprisingly, the gray whale does not feed on the surface of the ocean, but at the bottom! Down there it can scoop up extremely large amounts of water and mud and shellfish. Then the whale will filter the water and the mud out through its baleen plates, using its huge tongue, and swallow the remaining food.

Female gray whales are somewhat larger than males. The maximum length is about 50 feet and their weight can be as much as 45 tons.

The color of this type of whale is dark gray or black, but the mammal is usually covered with splotches, scars and barnacles. This causes the color to appear gray.

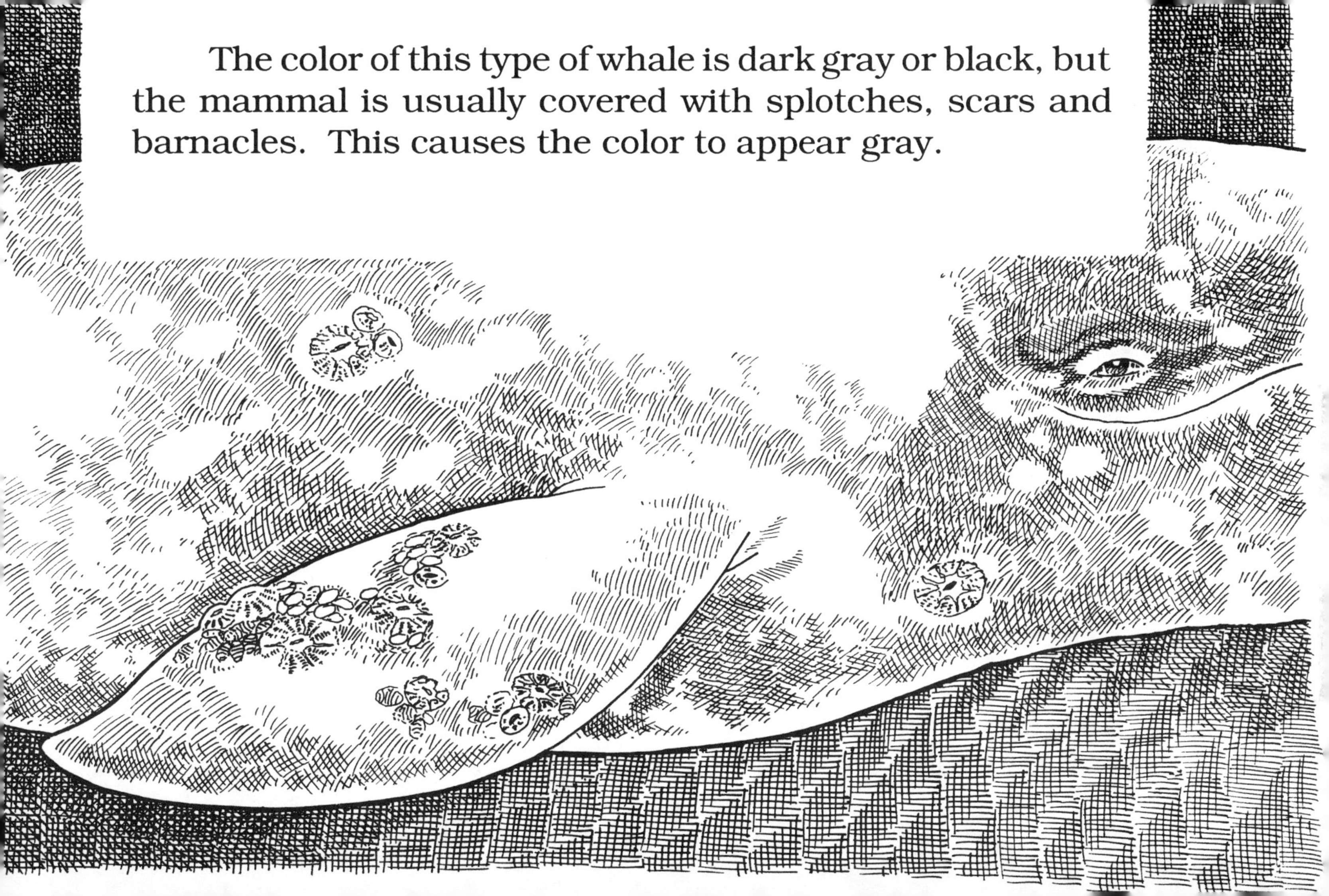

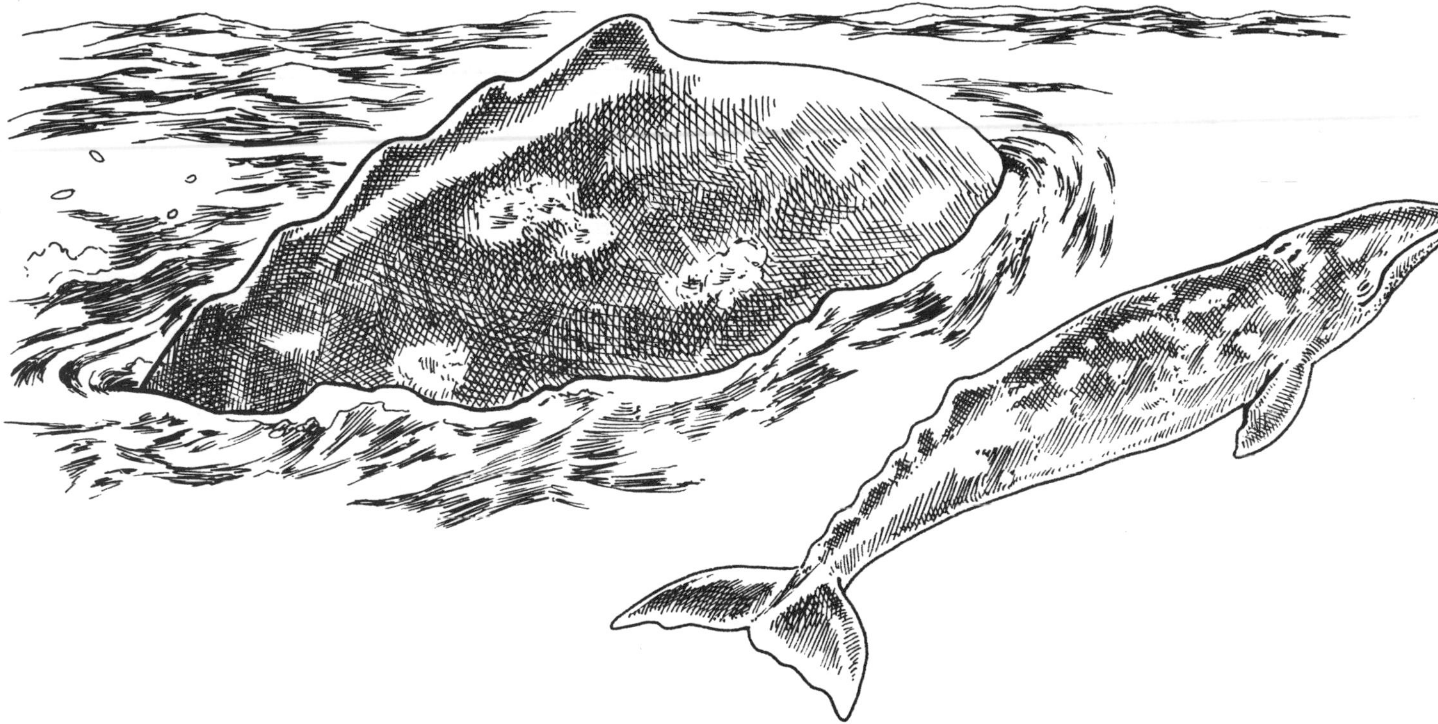

The gray whale is the only whale with a heavy mottled appearance, and it is also the only one with a bony ridge along its back.

As the whale swims, it moves its tail flukes up and down, pushing through the sea much the same as a human swimmer with her feet tied together.

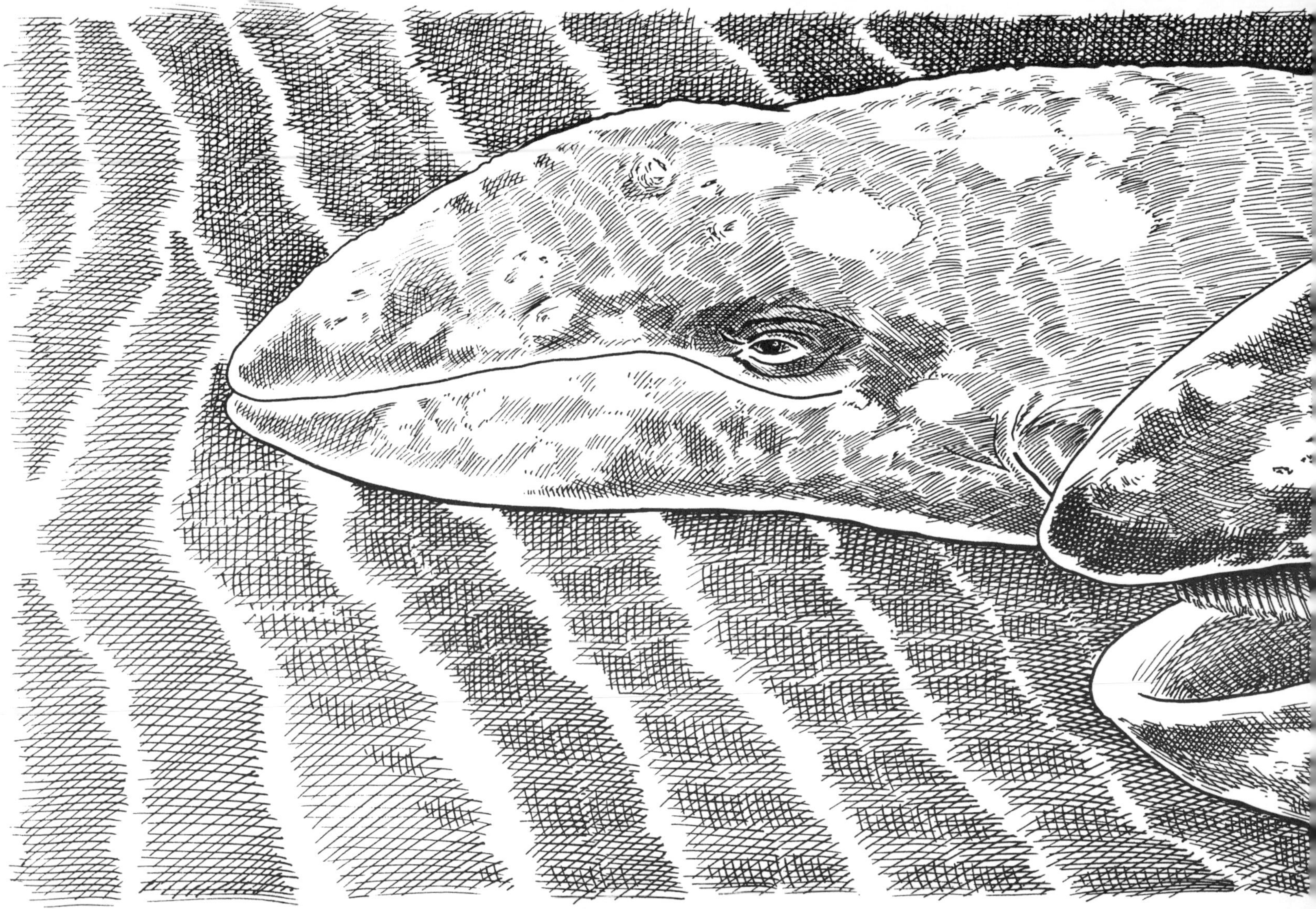

Whales have very good vision, but they depend on hearing and not on sight as they travel their long distances. Their eyes are on the sides of their heads and they can look straight forward as well as to the left and right.

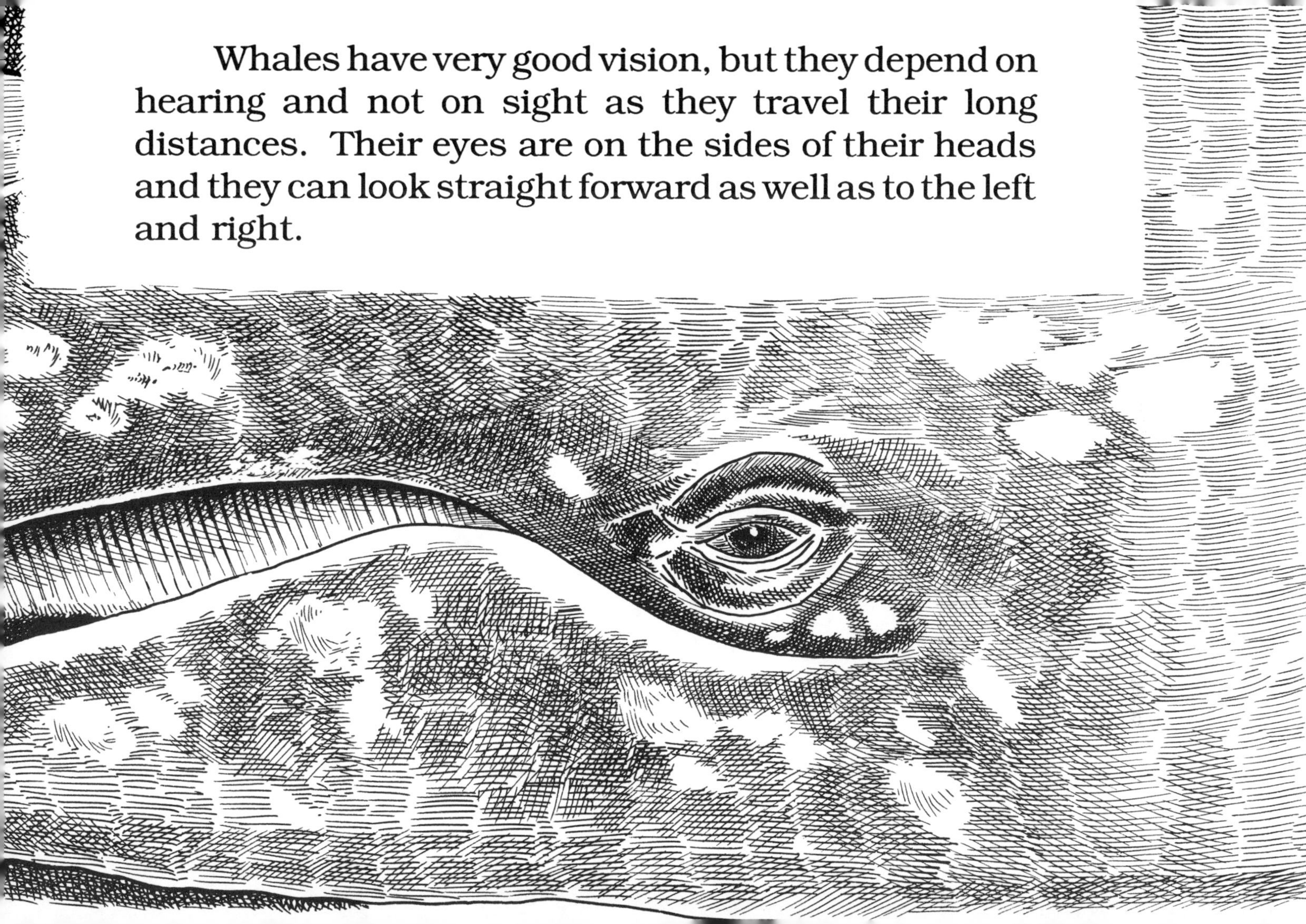

JUNE
JULY
AUGUST
SEPTEMBER
ALASKA
CANADA
UNITED STATES
MEXICO
BAJA CALIFORNIA
OCTOBER
NOVEMBER
DECEMBER
JANUARY
FEBRUARY
MARCH
APRIL
MAY
SOUTHERN MIGRATION of the GRAY WHALE

The gray whale makes the longest migration of any mammal. Its yearly round trip is over 10,000 miles, from the cold Bering Sea near Alaska to the warm lagoons in Baja California, Mexico.

They travel south, close to the shore, starting in the month of October. While these whales can be located almost any time of the year during their migration, they can best be viewed along the central California coast in December and January.

The gray whale does maintain a somewhat regular pace while migrating and it will breathe about four or five times each minute. It travels about 100 miles a day and it will take almost two months to complete its journey. It must keep moving almost twenty-four hours a day and, therefore, it has very little time for sleep. When the gray whale decides to submerge, it will toss its flukes in the air, swim under the water, and may remain there for about four minutes.

Females about to give birth arrive first in the lagoons, followed by males, and then the young of both sexes. It takes about thirteen and one-half months for a mother to produce a baby, and then only once every two or three years.

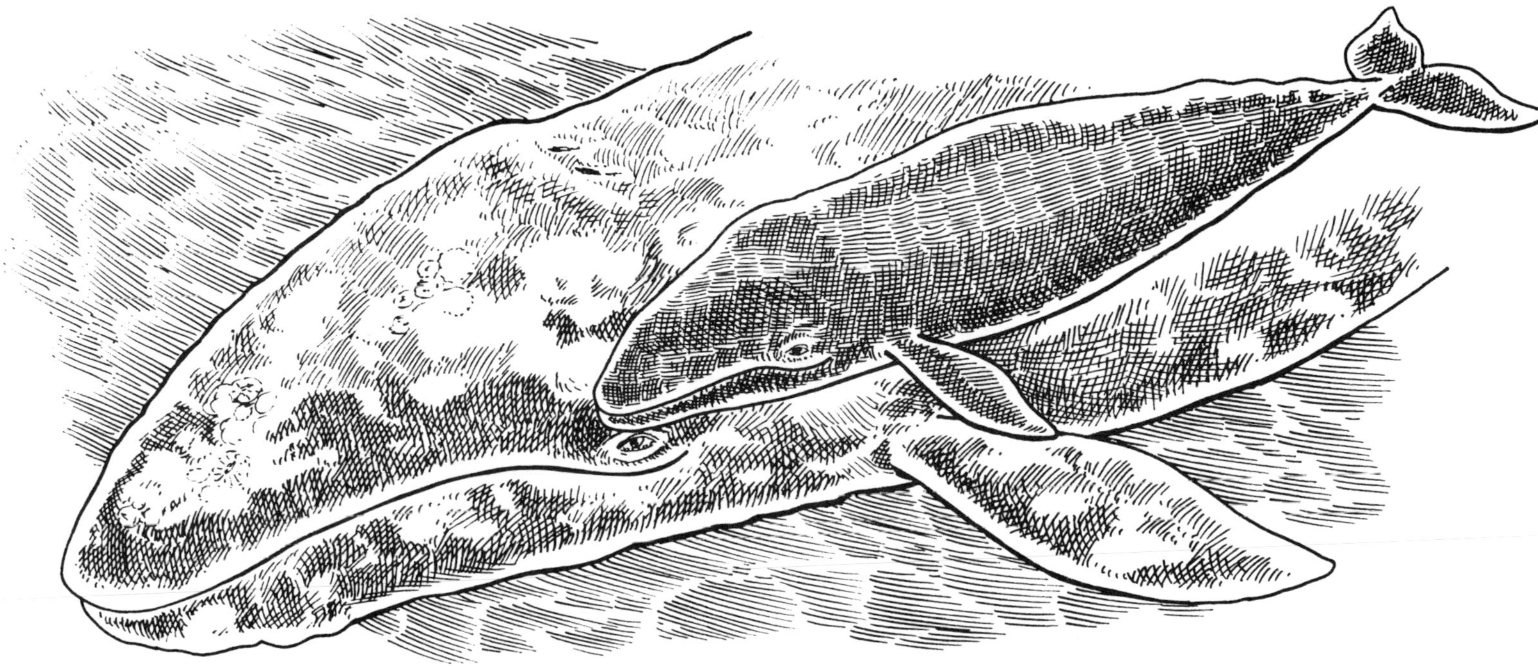

A lagoon is a small body of water partly separated from the sea by rocks or sand. The water is usually warm and shallow. Scientists think gray whales travel to give birth in the lagoons because it is easy to float there. A new-born whale, which has very little blubber to help it float, can swim much easier in the salty water of the lagoon.

The baby, called a calf, weighs about 1000 pounds at birth. It remains close to its mother, rolling over on her and splashing around while she stays calm. The baby takes milk, which is full of fat, protein and vitamins, from its mother the same way any other mammal does.

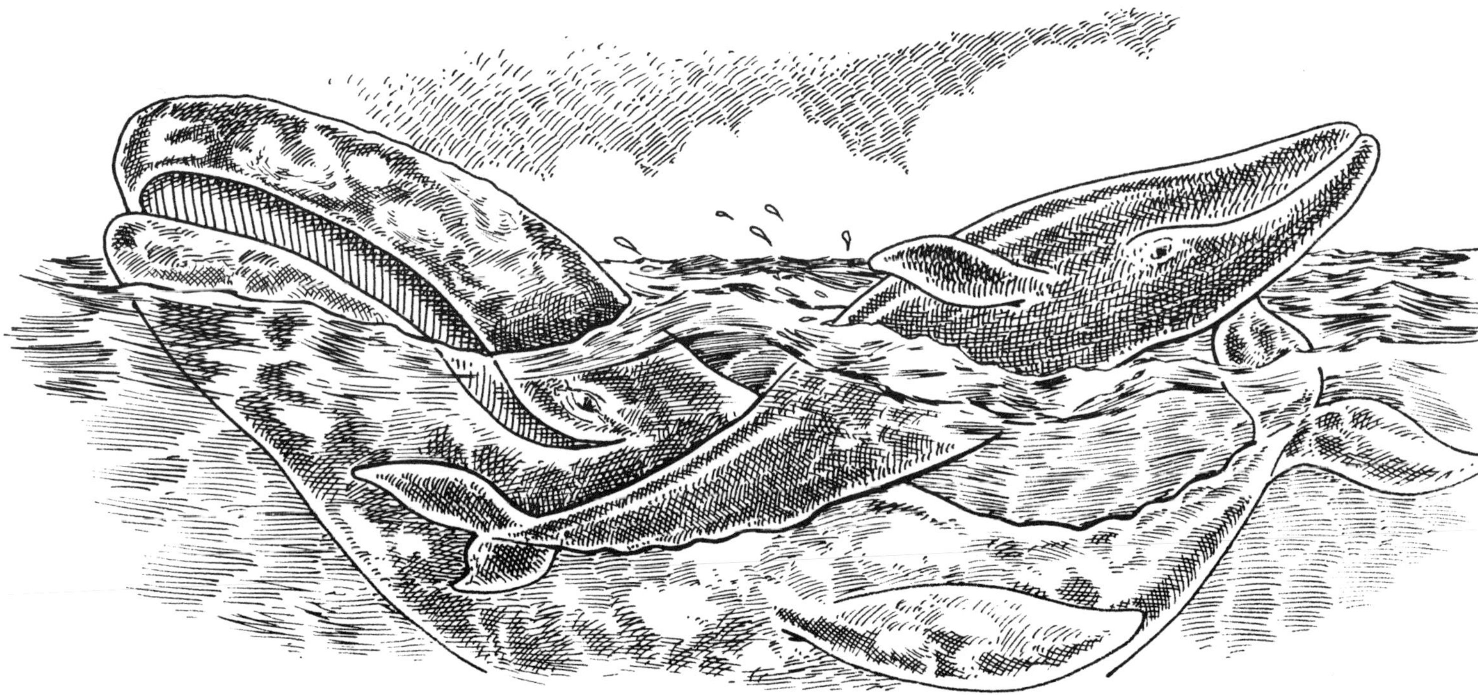

The calf will drink as much as 50 gallons of milk a day for almost seven months before eating the food of adults. It gains almost 250 pounds a day and the layer of blubber it grows will later give it protection against the icy waters of the Bering Sea.

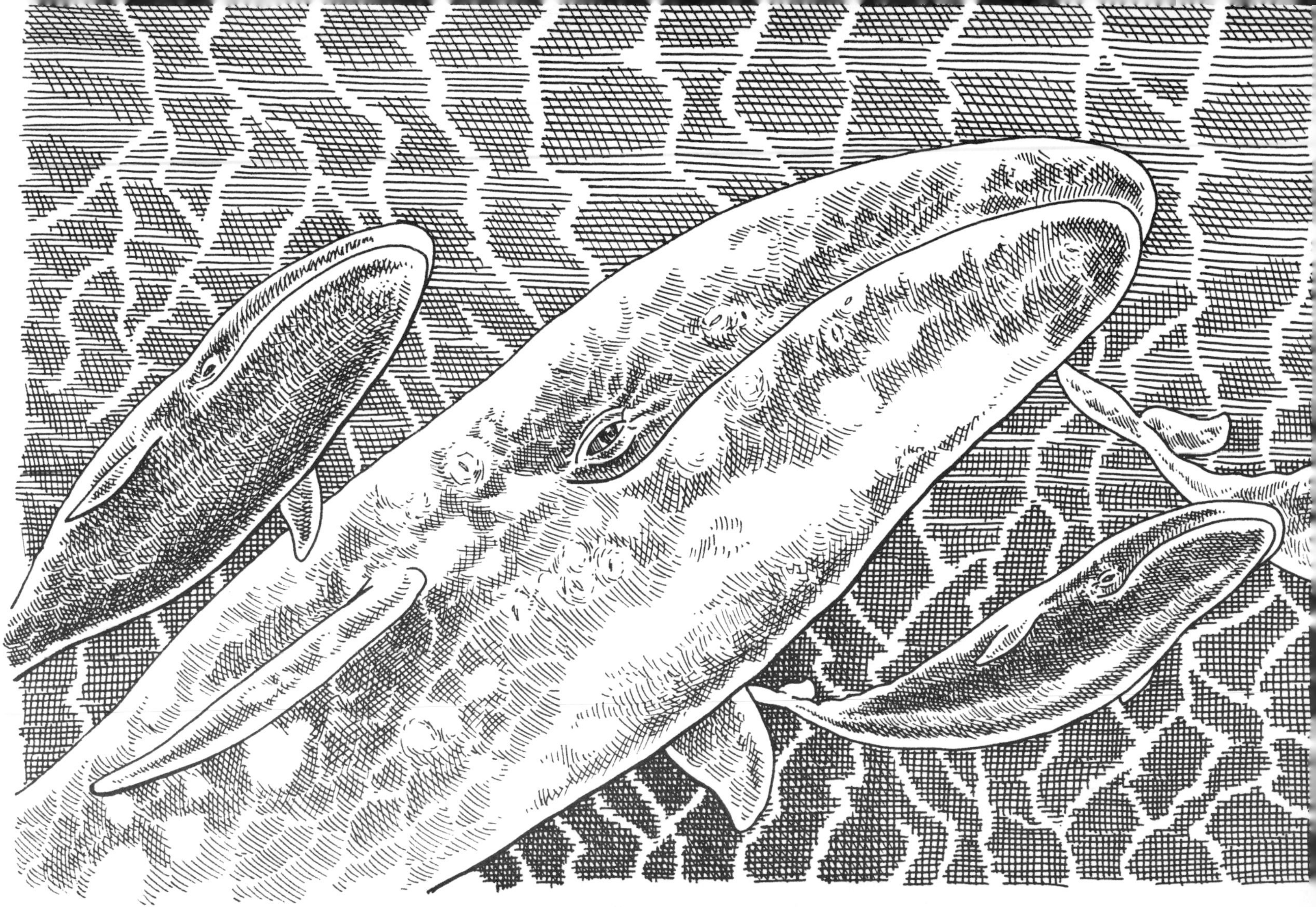

Gray whales are very protective of their calves and will defend them even if it might mean serious injury or perhaps death.

Gray whales make unusual sounds, as if they were talking with each other. Most sounds are made by the mother to her calf.

After spending two months in the lagoon breeding areas of Baja California, the whales begin the long journey north to Bering. They will arrive in May or June and stay for a four-month feeding period.

Gray whales often breach by throwing themselves almost completely out of the water and then landing on their side or back. No one knows why they breach, but it may be to attract a mate or just for having fun.

These whales sometimes "spy jump" by thrusting their heads high out of the water to look around and see where they are. This is a very unusual activity for so large a creature.

A gray whale's nostrils, called blowholes, are on top of its head. A new calf must learn to keep its two blowholes covered tightly when it swims below the surface or the water could get in and choke it.

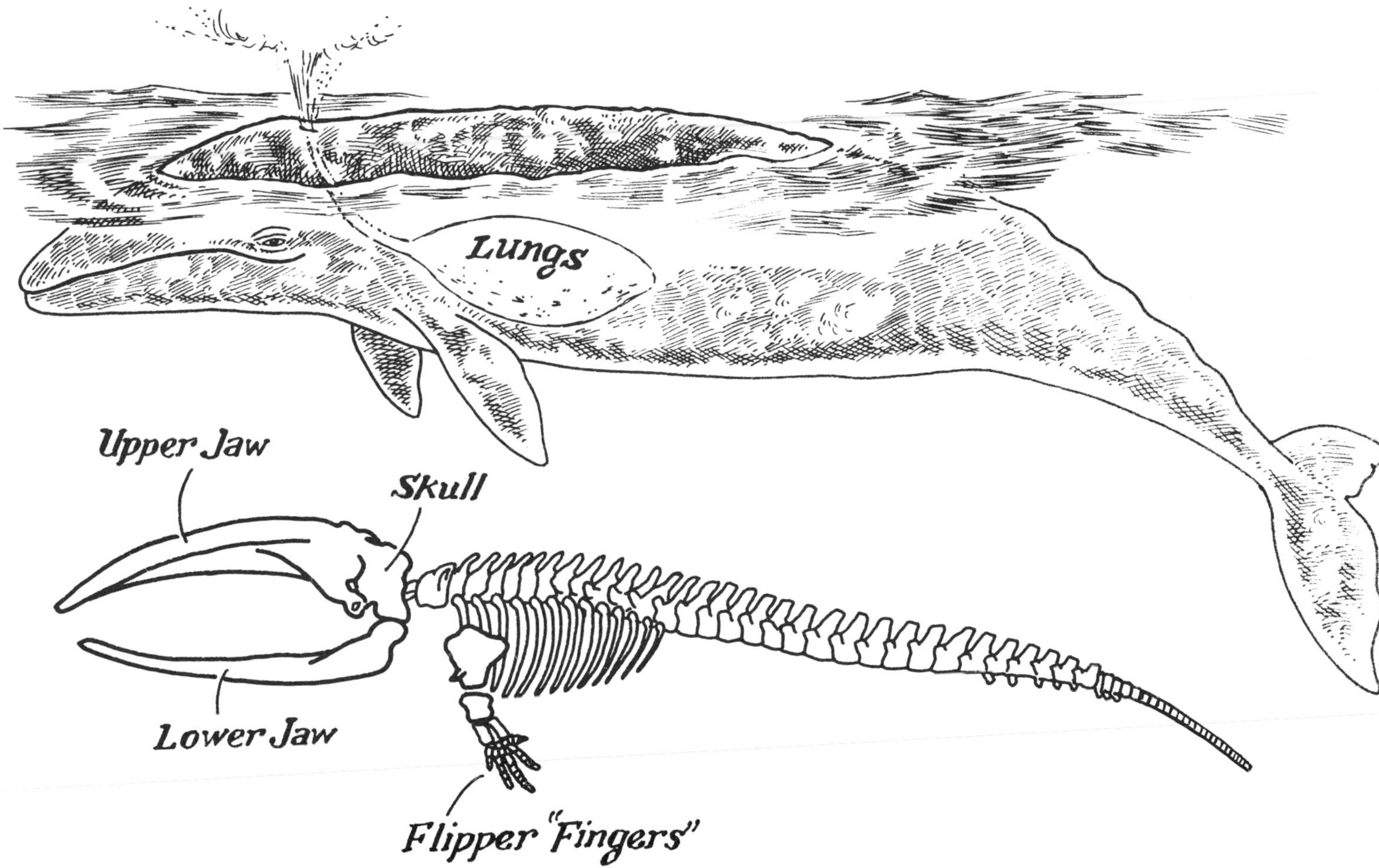
Lungs
Upper Jaw
Skull
Lower Jaw
Flipper "Fingers"

The gray whale's spout is visible when it comes to the surface to get some fresh air. The mammal spouts the stale air out of its blowhole with a WHOOSHING sound that can be seen and heard for a very long distance.

Scientists think that the spout is caused by the whale's warm, damp breath as it meets with the cooler air outside.

The only real danger in the sea which the gray whale might meet is the orca, usually named killer whale. The sound of the killer whale travels several miles and causes the gray whale to swim away quite rapidly. Sometimes the gray whale is so frightened by the killer whale it does not even struggle. The gray whale calves are easy prey for the killer whales and it is important for the mother to lead her baby as close to the shore as possible. A mother gray may not have enough experience to know this and will lead her baby though deep water. This is when the killers attack the young grays, especially in the Monterey Bay during the return trip to the Bering Sea from early April until early June.

The only danger out of the sea which the gray whale faces is man. In the days of whaling, so many gray whales were killed that by 1874 there were only about 8,000 left. Most of the females were taken in the shallow water of Scammon Lagoon in Baja. By 1914, it was believed that the gray whale was extinct!

The whales which survived were in places where man could not easily locate them and the population grew even though some whaling still took place. Now the gray whale is completely protected, and there is very little hunting of these mammals. In 1988, scientists indicated that there were more than 20,000 gray whales.

The California coastline provides an excellent place for viewing this giant mammal. Since the gray whale swims so close to the shoreline, it has become quite a tourist attraction. Whale-watching cruises allow interested people to follow the path of these mammals. However, it is most important to understand that new federal laws now require boats and people to stay at least 300 feet away from these gray whales.

BETTIE

This is an important law to respect, because too much disturbance in the route of the gray whales might cause them to migrate from one breeding area to another not quite so safe as their present destination.

It is wonderful and very special that these mammals are now protected so that future generations will have the privilege of watching and enjoying them.

AND NOW YOU KNOW WHAT A CALIFORNIA GRAY WHALE IS!

About the Author...

Dr. Jack A. Graves was involved in elementary education for thirty-five years: six as a teacher, five as a principal, and twenty-four as a university professor. He has a bachelor's degree from Arizona State University, and master and doctoral degrees from the University of California, Berkeley. He is now retired from teaching at California State University, Stanislaus and has been honored with the position of Professor Emeritus. He continues to enjoy observing the gray whales during their annual migrations along the coast of central California. He also visits elementary school classrooms to read his whale book to the children and to discuss the importance of animal conservation. He maintains an active interest in the International Reading Association, the California Reading Association, and the Stanislaus Reading Council. WHAT IS A CALIFORNIA SEA OTTER? is the title of his other children's book.

About the Artist...

Cameron K. Daines received his Bachelor of Science degree in Architectural Design from the University of Virginia. He has served as art director for KTGF-TV16 in Great Falls, Montana, and is currently pursuing a career in animation and freelance illustration. Cameron enjoys many fields of design, and is especially happy when his artwork serves to help children see and understand the beauty of the world about them.

About the Publisher...

American Educational Press specializes in educational, informative books for young people. Each title stimulates creative thinking and provides an adventure in learning!

Beaches Are For Kids!
Desert Discovery
Grand Canyon Discovery
Utah is for Kids!

Call or write for more information…
American Educational Press (a division of Double B Publications)
4113 N. Longview
Phoenix, Arizona 85014
(602) 274-7236